D0245727

THE ODD ONE OUT

THINGS THAT BEGIN WITH...

O E P R T W F S C D H A

On the next page, everything starts with c – all except one, which could it be?

Can you spot the **odd one out?**

The answer is...

THE
PARROT!

Which of these **shouldn't** be here?

The answer is...

THE TRUCK!

Can you spot the **odd one out?**

The answer is...

THE
MONKEY!

Which of these **shouldn't** be here?

The answer is...

THE

F̲ENCE!

Can you spot the **odd one out?**

The answer is...

THE BABY!

Which of these **shouldn't** be here?

The answer is...

THE
<u>H</u>EDGEHOG!

Can you spot the **odd one out?**

The answer is...

THE
PUMPKIN!

Which of these **shouldn't** be here?

The answer is...

THE
PEACOCK!

Can you spot the **odd one out?**

The answer is...

THE TRACTOR!

Which of these **shouldn't** be here?

The answer is...

THE
WATERING CAN!

Can you spot the **odd one out?**

The answer is...

THE SEAL!

Which of these **shouldn't** be here?

The answer is...

THE JELLYFISH!

Can you spot the **odd one out?**

The answer is...

THE CAT!

Which of these **shouldn't** be here?

The answer is...

THE
WIZARD!

Can you spot the **odd one out?**

The answer is...

Which of these **shouldn't** be here?

The answer is...

THE
<u>T</u>EDDY BEAR!

Can you spot the **odd one out?**

The answer is...

THE
KANGAROO!

BOOKS for little ONES

Find us on Amazon!

Discover all of the titles available in our store; including these below...